HEART'S GATE

Jargon 95

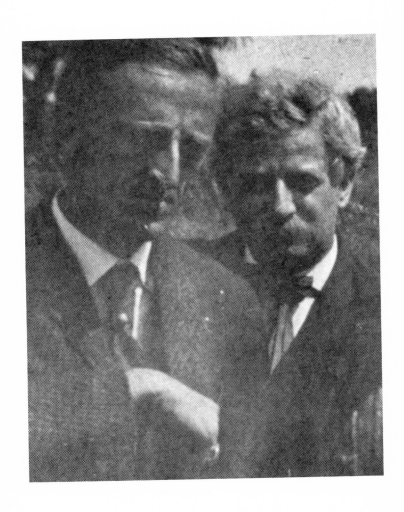

HEART'S GATE

Letters Between
Marsden Hartley & Horace Traubel
1906–1915

Edited & Introduced by
William Innes Homer

The Jargon Society
Highlands, North Carolina
1982

Support from *The National Endowment for the Arts,* a Federal agency, and the *John & Clara Higgins Foundation* is gratefully acknowledged.
The jacket design incorporates a photograph of Marsden Hartley's "Carnival of Autumn" (oil on canvas, 1908–09), and is reproduced courtesy of the *Museum of Fine Arts,* Boston. The image on the frontispiece is based on the only known photograph of Hartley and Traubel, taken at Green Acre, Maine, found in Mildred Bain's presentation copy—to her husband, Frank Bain—of her book on Horace Traubel, published in 1913 by Albert and Charles Boni, New York City. We would like to thank the present owner for the right to reproduction: Professor Cyril Greenland, School of Social Work, McMaster University, Hamilton, Ontario. And for calling our attention to the existence of the photograph, we thank: Professor Michael Lynch, Department of English, Erindale College, University of Toronto, Ontario.
Marsden Hartley's copy of *Leaves of Grass* is in the Special Collections department of the Kent State University Libraries, whom we thank for the reproduction supplied by Alex Gildzen.

Library of Congress Catalog Number: 81-86063
ISBN: 0-912330-48-1 (paper)

Printed by *Superior Printing,* Champaign, Illinois 61820
Designed by Alvin Doyle Moore
Manufactured in the United States of America
Distributed by
Inland Book Company
22 Hemingway Avenue
East Haven, Connecticut 06512

PREFACE

Marsden Hartley (1877–1943) is one of America's most distinguished artists. Any new information about him and his work deserves to be brought to the attention of the discerning public. Unexpectedly, I discovered a series of early letters by Hartley, presumed to be lost, and their content was so informative and revealing that I felt they should be published. The source of these letters was a longtime friend of our family, Gertrude Traubel, to whose father, Horace Traubel, Hartley had written them. She showed them to me in the mid-1970s, in connection with my research on the Stieglitz circle, and allowed me to make photographic copies of them at that time. In addition, several letters by Hartley, published here, were found in the Library of Congress.

About two years ago I discussed with Miss Traubel the idea of publishing these letters, and she was enthusiastic about the project and gave the necessary permission, for which I am very grateful. Moreover, at my request she furnished useful and important recollections of Hartley and her father, together with observations about some of the personalities mentioned in the letters. Much of this information has found its way into the notes, and for this I am once again in her debt.

What of the other side of the correspondence, that from Horace Traubel to Hartley? Gail Scott, who is editing Hartley's essays, told me she thought it existed but she did not know its where-abouts. A search revealed that it was housed in the Beinecke Rare Book and Manuscript Library at Yale University, and thanks to the kind permission of that institution and Hartley's niece, Norma Berger, I have been able to include many of Traubel's letters as well.

Although the exchange of correspondence between Hartley and Traubel covers a short span of years—1906–15—it is extraordinarily interesting on a number of counts. First of all, the letters stem from a time in Hartley's life about which very little has been known. From an art-historical standpoint alone they are valuable in telling us of Hartley's activities, aspirations, and artistic sources during his earliest phase as an independent artist. From a literary point of view his letters are among his most eloquent and poetic utterances, and they give us an intimate view of Hartley's inner life. Traubel's letters, too, function in much the same way, and allow us to see more profoundly into his deeply caring, sympathetic personality. The view of both sides of the correspondence, of course, gives us something unique and moving which separately they could never offer.

Traubel, nineteen years older than Hartley, had come to admire Whitman when the poet was living out his declining years in Camden, New Jersey. Becoming his friend, confidant, champion, and faithful recorder of his voluminous remarks, Traubel probably knew Whitman better than anyone else. After Whitman died in 1892, Traubel, based in Camden and Philadelphia, took on the responsibility of celebrating the poet's memory and message through his periodical *The Conservator* (published by my grandfather's firm), his independent writing and lecturing, and his formation of the Walt Whitman Fellowship International. With branches in several major American cities, the Fellowship sought to keep Whitman's spirit alive.

Before meeting Traubel in 1904 or 1905, Hartley was pursuing the challenging and absorbing task of becoming a painter. Born in Maine, he had studied in Ohio and New York before returning to his native state to paint as an independent artist just after the turn of the century. Although he had studied at the National Academy of Design, a stronghold of conservative art, Hartley soon turned enthusiastically toward the more advanced language of Impressionism and Neo-Impressionism, and through his knowledge of these styles endeavored to become a modernist. Such a course was ultimately to bring him artistic success as an avant-garde painter and a certain amount of fame during his lifetime, but in his earlier years Hartley's unconventional style made it very difficult for him to earn money through the sale of his work. As a result, his struggle to grow and develop as an artist was compounded by continuing economic woes. Both concerns, accordingly, permeate his letters to Traubel.

In writing to Traubel, Hartley was addressing a beloved hero and a mentor. Just how or why his deep affection for Traubel developed is unknown, but clearly the older man meant a great deal to the artist as a dear friend, sounding board, and source of advice and inspiration. Hartley had come to admire Whitman and his writings, and that interest, too, would have guaranteed a bond between the two men. Indeed, the quality of their relationship owes much, I believe, to Whitman's concept of comradeship or "adhesiveness" between sympathetic souls. From the letters it appears, however, that the affection that flowed from Hartley to Traubel was rather more intense than from Traubel to Hartley.

Beside revealing much about the relationship and individual aspirations of both Hartley and Traubel, the correspondence tells us something of the progressive artistic, literary, and social milieu to which both men belonged. There are glimpses of Dodge Macknight, Philip Hale, Desmond Fitzgerald and the Boston art world; Thomas Bird Mosher and Dr. Percival Wiksell of the Whitman circle; Mrs. Ole Bull, the generous patron who helped Hartley and other young artists; and the intellectual-mystical colony of Green Acre at Eliot, Maine, with its roster of dedicated adherents such as Charlotte Perkins Gilman and Helen Campbell.

The period covered by these letters is relatively short, but the frequency with which Hartley and Traubel wrote each other gives a special intensity and richness to the correspondence. There is also a directness of feeling, a deep humanity, a willingness to commit everything to the cause of art that makes these letters extraordinarily revealing documents of artistic life in early twentieth-century America.

William Innes Homer
Wilmington, Delaware
March 1, 1982

EDITOR'S NOTES

The letters of Marsden Hartley and Horace Traubel are published here almost without alteration. I have had to correct a misspelled word or proper name here and there, but other than that the wording of the letters remains untouched. Because Hartley often omitted punctuation, it has been introduced in brackets whenever the meaning of the letter urgently demanded it; otherwise, the flow of the letters has been left as it was in the original.

Hartley's and Traubel's letters also presented another problem: they were often very difficult to decipher. Therefore, if I had doubts about the identity of a word, I indicated that by a question mark or an alternative reading in brackets. A few words and phrases were totally illegible and were so indicated. Some of the letters were not dated, but the postmark on the envelope often gave the month, day, and year of mailing. This information has been included whenever it was available. In a few cases I have placed undated letters in the chronological sequence on the basis of internal evidence.

Virtually every letter and postal card in the two-way correspondence has been printed in the following pages. In a few instances, short notes on totally practical matters were omitted because they added nothing to our understanding of Hartley and Traubel.

Notes at the end of the letters define and amplify the identity of known individuals and events mentioned therein. I am grateful to Suzi Isaacs for her assistance in securing such information and for helping me transcribe the letters.

No information has been found about the following individuals mentioned in the letters: Bloomfield, Miss Drew, Edith Howell, Fred Lunt, Harlan Ober. "Sanger" may be a reference to Margaret Sanger.

W. I. H.

Boston
15th Aug '06

Dear Hartley—
Your yesterday's note is here. I am sorry we are not to see you. The devil has shuffled our cards against us. But we will meet south later, in the winter if we can do no better. I shall be glad to hear that you are returned from Lewiston, which seems to depress your spirit. The Fiske[?] people certainly treated you rather oddly. No doubt you can hit[?] something if you can get down to N.Y. But you should get there at once. We return to N.Y. on Friday's boat. If you can see yourself through[?] to Boston Friday I will see you through to N.Y. including the grub. We could go down together. You can get no stateroom— possibly—it's so late—but you could get a mattress, which I have often accepted myself. I expect to see you arrived in N.Y. so you can make an immediate try with the managers. If I wasn't all bound & knotted up myself I would say "here take this," & spill the dollars over you. I hurry you this note right in the wake of yours just here. Love to you.

Traubel

Borrow enough to get here & I
will see you the rest of the
way. Don't hesitate. I'd let
you do such things for me if I needed them &
you could do them.

Phila
25 Aug '06

Dear Hartley:

I have had two letters from you since I came home. I am in luck. The work I find to do here is even worse accumulated than I expected. I got down to business at once. I am not sure that a lot of the "important" things we do are worth while anyway—better not done than done. Still, I work on & ask no questions. I cannot do more than send you snatches of talk—words here & there as the days pass. Advise you? I could not do it. What your soul finally sets you doing I know will get done well. Do not doubt your soul. I would not be sorry to learn that you were in New York, where I might see you occasionally. But I shall understand & yell "hurrah" if you find a better service[?] possible in Lewiston & stay there. Give my love to the girl. Tell her to write me. And as for you—well I don't need to say old things over again.   Lovingly—

Traubel

Boston
Oct 26 '06

I am back here & may stay until the end of next week.
Your last letter has been forwarded to me. Do not doubt me.
I am glad to receive your letters. I can't always answer in full
or off hand but my heart makes a lot of you & cherishes the
fact of your good will. I wish you could [illegible word] down
while I am in Boston but I suppose that is impossible. Yes,
you have your troubles. But troubles belong with the norm of
life. We get into trouble but we do not stay in. We went last
night to see Hansell in Theodora & today Paul Ahrendt was
in to see Wiksell.[1] When I see actors I think of you. Indeed,
when I do not see actors I think of you, too. Love fills my heart
& you are in my heart.

Traubel

To Hartley

My Dear Horace.

I received your recent letter from Boston and it is somewhat of a surprise to learn that you are there, so near at hand and yet millions of miles away, as far as the possibility of seeing you is concerned. Tho' I do not doubt you, neither do I mean to expect too much of you for you have countless things to keep you busy whereas I have nothing but my own thoughts and these keep me in one continuous quandary as to how to survive the insweep of the sea of uncertainties. I hope sincerely and if I were a praying man, I should pray most fervently to be released from these harrowing doubts. Assurances are much better things to hold and I am trying my best to hold them. I do not expect unreasonable things but I find it so damnably difficult to acquire just the reasonable necessities. However I am one in millions and it is of little consequence from the world point of view. It seems to me though that I never have needed a chance quite so much as I do now for my whole future would almost seem to depend upon the privilege of seeing the winter. I shall do the best I can though and try and not complain. I would give much if I could run in at the doctor's [Dr. Percival Wiksell] to see you and see him, and just be with you both. I don't think you realize either of you the benefit to me just to be in the presence of those who know what an ambition, what a desire is, to feel the importance of something else beyond the eating and sleeping. I confess to a very human appetite for both, but yet it is not my entire life. I do not suffer for either of these just now but still I find everything resolves into compromises and I hate them.

I am glad for the late message from you and I am always happy in spreading you about whenever the opportunity affords itself. Will you give the doctor my very kindest regards. I have much admiration for him and I don't think he fully realizes the powers of his personality or possibly he does. I hope so at any rate. If he does or doesn't he won't mind being told of it. He has one of those roomy hearts which the world needs. I hope when I write you again I can offer something more pleasant, more relieving. I know so little of the world's affairs, and what I know comes from a heart that has felt more the sorrow than the gladness and so my views lean[?] a little too much upon the violet or the gray to get at the crimson or the gold. This first snow-storm of ours here is just a pleasant reminder of the lovely things I hope to see here during the winter for Maine is where nature does beautiful things in winter. My love to you, I hope that you are finding things more to your tastes and ambitions. You never talk of yourself and your doings with the dullness that I do—you have a happy way of making all moments bright. Let me hear from you when you can share a moment. Lovingly

Hartley

Undated letter, postmarked November 2, 1906, Lewiston, Maine

My Dear Horace.

I am wondering what has become of you since I last heard from you in Boston. I have presentiments occasionally that make me feel you are tussling with the problems. That seems to be the chief business of all of us who want to do things[,] doesn't it? You may be interested to learn that I have finally succeeded in getting a studio and am working hard to make a go of teaching here and painting by myself. I want so much to turn out something this winter that will be worthy of my desires and just now I am doing some things to send to New York in view of possible sales. I have a friend there who kindly offers services in my behalf and she may be able to realize something for me. My subjects here in Maine are naturally most attractive and I am working to make worthy studies of them. I have one study of the river here at night with a lot of buildings jutting out over the river. Ice(?) in the frosty glow of a cold winter night, very cold indeed, several degrees below zero, the kind of night when the air fairly cuts one's flesh yet at the same time invigorates. Then another study of sunset glow through the pine woods with the first snow on the ground in patches left where the day sun has not reached there much. I have a very happy faculty of being able to work very rapidly so that I am able to seize very readily upon the most striking characteristics of a subject. I am banking on the teaching business to pay expenses and upon my pictures to relieve other pressures. I did want very much to send something to the Pennsylvania Academy [of the Fine Arts] but the time is too short before pictures must be in and I could not send anything there that doesn't display my real powers, and so of course I shall not send, but I hope to get something ready for the New York Exhibition in February or March. I felt that you would be a little interested in hearing of me and I would dearly love to hear something of you. The winter effects up here are so beautiful, so unusual and attractive, the lovely contrasts of the sober green of the pines and the velvety purples of the deciduous growth with the simple big masses of snow stretching about into infinity. Love and very best wishes to you.

> Marsden Hartley
> Greely Building Suite 4.
> Lewiston Maine.

The songs of the sleigh bells ring ever pleasantly in my ears and recalling happily some of my childhood days.

I enclose you one of my primitive hand-made announcements.

Undated letter, postmarked December 6, 1906, Auburn, Maine

EDMUND·MARSDEN·HARTLEY·
·New York·
Announces ·· classes · in ·
drawing · and · painting · in ·
all · mediums · oil · water —
color · charcoal · black · and ·
white · drawing · from · the ··
antique (cast) · and · from · life ·
A · special · all · day · class ··
will · be · held · on · Saturdays ·
in · his · studio · THE · GREELY ·
BUILDING · 171 · LISBON · ST ·
SUITE · FOUR · ❯❯❯

Arrangements · may · be · made ·
for · classes · on · other · days ·

Invitation, hand-made by Marsden Hartley

Phila
Feb 7 '07

    I do not forget, dear Hartley. But things here hold me down tight on the earth. I too have problems. I don't cry over them. Nor do you. But I find myself at my wits' end to keep my pulse regular. I may be in Boston towards the end of next month. I am hoping you may be moving South by that time. You must not stay in Maine too long. Do your work there. Then shake fur[?]—come back into the crowd. Are you painting some this winter? I never forgot the strong canvasses you showed me. I am forced to work hard on the Conservator.[2] And then my fingers wear through & make the work harder or delay me day after day. December is [illegible words]. But—all the stars are left in my sky. I send you my love.

Traubel

Horace Traubel.

I am happy my dear Horace, to receive a message out of the thick of things and from the depths of the heart. I have received from time to time with such joy, the Conservators and have by me now the two copies of December. I am certain that the world cannot get on, or get on as easily, without its Conservator. It needs its Traubel voice as we who are perhaps a little bit nearer to you by reason of direct friendship need it. I have satisfied myself in the long silence since I was last in your stimulating presence, with the words in the Collects[3] which seemed <u>said</u> to me perhaps a wee bit more than to the others in the world, and I have thoroughly contented myself with them knowing one day I should receive direct communication from the heart of you by letter and here I have it—I have talked with you many times by photo process and now I look at you straight ahead of me, and say it is just good to know you. I know I ought to come down out of the woods, and few know how much I need the crowd and love it—God knows I want to be with it and near it always—for I loathe being apart either from my crowd or my mountains and just now I am both, except in my pictures and then I am happily contented to be climbing the heights and the clouds by the brush method when I cannot do it actually by body and soul. I would be happy if I could show you my later efforts at rendering the God-spirit in the mountains: Others like them who have seen them, and I am confident you would. I have had the joy of having for my spectators some woodsmen, men who know mountains and clouds profoundly as a result of daily intercourse with them and they are unanimous in their praise and appreciation—one says he thinks the same kind of big things when he looks at my mountains that he does when looking at God's, so I am complimented.

I have been digging persistently on three or four fairly good size canvases (25 x 30) and these are to go to the Exhibition of The National Academy in New York for their March show, that is if they get by, and I feel convinced that at least one will.—

If you come Bostonwards then, will you not be able to find an hour to look me up there and see what they have done to me? I have to rely wholly on friends for this information and I should feel proud if I knew you went to look at me in my mountains. I sent five small ones (16 x 20) down to Wiksell to look at, and I am surprised in knowing he has changed his course—but this is what the world does to us all—it makes us swing about all ways that we may discover the straight way. As much as I need the crowd, I do not see myself in it before next fall at any rate and <u>then</u>, I cannot see so far away. I am however, happy that I am digging [dragging?] out of the uncertainties a chance to put myself up before the public and I am enjoying the privilege of working, of finding expression— for this is what we all must have—a channel through which to give ourselves out to those about us and near to us. I am curious to see what my public appearance will do for me or to me. I am not over-expectant, yet I anticipate a little: Your voice is a joyful sound to my soul and when I cannot hear it nearly as much as I desire I content myself with occasional breakings of silence as when in the depths of the mountains the eagle flies above one's head, and the loon calls out to the heart, and makes the silence sweeter. My love, all of it to you my dear Horace; I think much and often of you, see your maimed and bruised fingers and feel the throbbing of your pulses, but never a quaver in the song. I spread you round in my every chance and you do not pass unheard even here in the desert of factories and relinquished ambitions, where souls seem dead and bodies look famished and worn.

Let me hear you when you can again as I like your voice and need it. Your comrade-lover.

Edmund Marsden Hartley.

Greely Bldg.
Suite 4
Lewiston Maine.

Undated letter, Postmarked February 10, 1907

Bost.
Mar 28 '07

I wish you were here. Love to you. I walk these streets &
seem to have you at my side. I say about this poem: make it so
it will mean something to the general readers.[4] I know what
you mean because you tell me but I find that other people
I hand it to are completely mystified. I do not criticize the
writing. But in publishing such a thing it should be made
general & enough[?] concrete in its clues to lead the student
to a result. Love to you. Write me. Yes, I wish you were here.

Traubel

Phila
July 3d '07

Dear Hartley:

Yes, I hope to see you at Greenacre in August. Meanwhile
stroke the tater-bottoms with your wise palm[?] & try to give
them[?] some sense. Helen Campbell is an oasis in a desert.
She springs eternal in that land of the dear dead. She is vital.
I was repaid & paid over if by no more than meeting her
[illegible words] As a matter of fact there are always some
people in such a settlement to redeem it. You'll probably find
Bloomfield there in his camp. He is worth more than White[?].
See all you can of him. I don't write much, dear brother. But
my heart does not forget. I have just got the May paper done
& must do some on July before I go off. I work hard enough to
get done but don't always get all the real things done. That's
the way I am so short in my correspondence. Your little board
is up over my desk—the office here: Revere Beach: it takes me
back to fine times we had together last summer. Good night!
You will hear from me again.

Love to you.
Traubel

My Dear Horace

I should have written you long ago but I am busy and leisure for writing seems a scarcity. Am having the most beautiful experiences with dear Mrs. Campbell.[5] She is certainly a choice personality of the fullest type rich in the richest things.

Affairs here move in the customary manner[;] much useless matter exhibited, but the real intentions of the place are the highest. I do hope you will give us as much of your time as you can. We are already counting the days. Bloomfield, the dearest of men, returned to Boston today and already I miss him. I have been prevented from having a full taste of his nature by all sorts of interfering personalities around him so have not gotten all I wish of him, but I shall see him again and shall write him.

I am spreading your thoughts everywhere at every opportunity by the Conservator and am doing you some service. I wish I could pull in the subscribers for you, but they don't pull like that. They have to come of themselves. All my love to you and Mrs. Campbell's too for I know she has it for you.

Marsden Hartley

Undated letter, postmarked July 25, 1907, Eliot, Maine.

Boston
Aug 13 '07

It was just right for us all to get together on that spot. We will not forget. Time will pass. We will not forget. Sorrows will come. Triumphs will come. We will not forget. Love tucks all its experience away somewhere. Draws upon it divinely in days of need. Is never thwarted. It was just right for us all to get together on that spot. We will not forget.

Traubel

To Hartley

Boston
Thursday

Dear Hartley—
    Wiksell & I expect to go up to Hampton Sunday afternoon. We may telephone & try to get you to meet us in the ev'g either at Portsmouth or Hampton. Mrs. Campbell came, we saw & she conquered.

Love to you.

Horace

Undated letter, postmarked August 15, 1907, Boston, Mass.

Horace Traubel

My Dear Horace

Your two letters of love are here[,] the last with the lovely postal picture just in my hands; also your fine photo before me. I read your letters to my dear friends because your words ring like heavensongs in the ears of all listeners.

The fulnesses come flooding over me like gusts of rose aromas and I am a bit overcome with the fragrances of them. This week in your absence we have had the joy of having Charlotte Perkins Gilman[6] and she has avowed her likings for me and for Harlan Ober, one of the highest of heaven born boys, and has shared herself with us without restrictions (when she has been a closed volume to many others)—for which gods be praised. I want Harlan Ober to have the divine privilege of knowing you one day. Also the other member of our perfect trinity, Fred Lunt, who has the eyes of a very god and a smile of the mothers of gods upon him. Place me in the middle between these two lovers of mine and there you have us. I will send you our pictures one day. The little Kodak photos taken by Sanger are very decent[,] one especially fine of Wiksell and Helen Campbell. I will also send you these. Please be sure and telephone me in good time on Sunday[,] say at one o'clock so I will know when to meet you. I want every one of these celestial minutes with you both. How near you both are, I have no words, only gods within us shall tell of my love for both of you. It is superb to have you both getting divinely nearer to the throne of my being. I mean rather, you are already there waiting to be taken and you are drawn in wholly. With Helen C.[,] Horace Traubel, Percival Wiksell, Charlotte Gilman, Harlan Ober, Fred Lunt, all these golden glories of my heart's gate. How can I contain myself. Let the word love tell it all and let me be happy in the sound of it and all the echoes and the semitones of it along with the full chords. Heavens are at my feet and gods look into my eyes and I am consumed with their glories.

Love for each and all.

Marsden Hartley

Undated letter, postmarked August 16, 1907, Eliot, Maine.

Marsden Hartley circa 1906

Boston
Aug 17 '07

Dear brother:
    Don't rate me so high. Keep me well on the ground. Don't
put a fancy price on me. Figure out its cost—without profits.
You really talk big about us because you are big yourself. Your
eye sees big. That is beautiful. But it is hard on us. It makes
us seem like frauds. It makes us feel as if we cavorted about
under false names & were credited with false measurements.
I want your love. You have mine. But I don't want you to make
me handsome or large. That's not me.

Traubel

My Dear Horace.

Enclosed find subscription for Conservator with the address below. We are all working for the Conservator's good and I think you are taking root in a set of new hearts here who find your words music in their souls. Am having divine times with the soul relations of my dear brothers Ober and Lunt of whom I have spoken before. They are superb fellows and I want them to pass into your life for their sakes, so I speak of them as I write. When you come here again which is to be I hope soon, I wish to have Ober meet you. I see the mail carrier coming down the field so must close this for now. Waited patiently for your phone message yesterday P.M. Love to Wiksell and yourself.

M. Hartley

Send Conservator to
International Working People's
    Social Center
88 Charles Street
Boston

Undated letter, postmarked [month illegible, August?] 19, 1907, Eliot, Maine.

My Dear Horace.

Enclosed find another subscription for the Conservator with the address below.

I love your letters and all your words but I refuse to be corrected for my estimations. I see nothing through colored glasses nor through a dark mirror. I know what I see and my heart corroborates my sight. Therefore you must stand as I feel you to be. There is no fraudery nor over measurement. I take the exact sizes of all people whether of my near kinship or no. The fulness of my love goes with this to the men whom I love so much. Send me as many words as you can while you are nearer me. Love from Helen C., Ober and myself, Ober especially.

M. Hartley

Mrs. Emma Newcomb
20 St. Paul Street
Cambridge Mass.

Undated letter, postmarked August 20, 1907, Eliot, Maine.

Boston
Aug 21 '07

Dear Hartley:

The two letters were here in my mail. The money I can make use of. The love ditto. The money I will make use of today. The love will last out days & years. I was glad to see you again. Glad to see our great mother. Glad to sit by you on the bare boards & look off up the river[?]. Glad to read, sitting in front of your tent, the sun going down, the beautiful afternoon passing away in an atmosphere of anthems & hallelujahs. Glad you went to Portsmouth with us & broke bread & [illegible word] with us & only said "auf wiedersehen" when you had to. The story is not all told. But this is a happy chapter.

Traubel

Boston
Aug 28 '07

Dear brother:

This is your great week. I think the sun is just shining for you this week. That the stars shine for you. And that love is in my heart for you. This is your week. And though the world accords you no victory and yet your heart will emerge from the sunbeams remade & sufficient. I shall not forget my dear pilgrimages to the north. The counterfeit journeys will all vanish. But these genuine conventions of the spirit will never be sponged out. We will meet again. Meet soon. Yes: and meet in love. I do not doubt but you are opening the doors today upon a beautiful prospect. I stand by your side rejoicing in your achievements. Dear brother!

Traubel

Boston Aug 29 '07

Love to you all at Greenacre.[7] I hate Greenacre & I love it. God made it magnificent. It's the business of somebody there to back up God. I shall never be sorry to remember that Greenacre is a fact. There are the best of reasons for thinking the worst of it. And there are also the best of reasons for cherishing its sacred intimations. I do not go much for the pale saviors. I like my saviors to have red faces & passions. To walk about on strong feet. To have appetites & to be proud of their bodies. A few of you at Greenacre save the place. But for you it would wash out in the first storm. I send you my love. I go away to the south. But I take precious memories with me. Love to you all.

Traubel

Dear Hartley

Your words my dear Horace have never been richer than now. It is my week and the gods walk close by me and with your face, the faces of my other brothers Ober and Lunt, adding also that superb countenance of our dearest Helen Campbell, I scarcely know what more I need. There is fellowship existing between us such as does not happen with every turn of the wheel. My exhibition is a splendid success artistically, financially very encouraging with future prospects most promising. Today Sunday is to be <u>the</u> day; Mrs. Mary Lucas of Boston, who has a most exquisite voice, is to sing for me, a Miss Fuller of Brooklyn is to play some MacDowell numbers. Lend us your presence. I would be too happy to see you walking about among my landscapes, lending your radiances, spreading your glows about us all.

I write you here at the desk of our Helen Campbell with Lunt at the piano playing softly, "Don' you cry ma honey" and singing beautifully, with Helen C. and Harlan Ober on the couch. I give you a touch of this atmosphere because it is beautified by sweetest memories of you. The couch near me seems even to creak with your sixteen ounces to the pound upon it, and I feel you so near me and imagine if I look back I shall surely find you sitting there in the body, but I am not looking[,] for I wish not to be deceived.

Your messages of love are precious, invaluable to my soul and I want every least word you can send out of your busyness. Send me the paper you spoke of that Walt [Whitman] used to send out, also the autograph, anything that you know will add to my joy. I would so love to have the manuscript of "Do you help me to live" Collect. We read it again here yesterday and there, superb things in it. You know I could seldom ask you for things like this, but if you felt like sending them, I should be ineffably happy. I remember with joy those last moments with you on the train[,] your arm about me feeling the love throbs passing over me and the parting was so filled with beauty and promise. When I think of the days and years to come, getting nearer and nearer to you as love brings us together. It is enough to live.

I am glad for your real thoughts on Green Acre. I am glad you like to see the possibilities, to count them at their true value. There are fine things in the air for the future of this place and we look forward to many real things for this spot. God has breathed heavily on these acres and we want the Godbreath to stay. My love, the fullest, deepest richest of it is yours. Lunt, Ober and Helen Campbell send theirs.

Marsden Hartley

Alfred E. Lunt [signed]   Harlan F. Ober [signed]

Helen Campbell [signed]

Undated letter, postmarked September 2, 1907, Eliot, Maine.

Phila
Sept 3d '07

Hartley, dear brother:

I am hard pushed & buried deep in accumulated work but I think I can still yell hello in a voice you may hear. Maine is not so far from Pennsylvania—when love claims the right of way. I visit you in body & spirit. You all belong to me whether you will or no. And I hope I belong to you. That is for you to say. Philadelphia is tropical. I go back to the shore today until Monday. Love!

Horace

Asbury Park
Sept 8 '07

Dear Hartley:

I am here with the folks again. We are still having summer down this way. I don't know whether it is right to address you now at Greenacre. Do not neglect to inform me of any change you make in your habitat. You will not doubt my constant thought of you: my eyes look back & about me & ahead & you are always within sight. This summer Greenacre has given me hallowed associations. I love you all with all my love & I send you my how do you do across the States.

Traubel

Phila
Sept 9 '07

Dear brother:

I hear from Sanger that you have almost certainly decided to settle in Boston. I had hoped to have you nearer me—and I have thought New York might open more doors to you. But I will see you sometime anyway. Love to you always. You don't need me. You need yourself. You will climb on the ladder of your self. Bless you.

Horace

Horace Traubel and Dr. Percival Wiksell

I am glad my dear Horace for your latest words of thought and love. I have not the least concern over your constant thought of me. I know I do play a part in your days' round and you play a continuous part in the circuit of the hours and days with me.

We are deliciously quiet here by ourselves Helen Campbell, Harlan Ober and myself. Last week was another gala week among us comrades in love. Fred Lunt spent the entire week with us and nothing intervened to mar the completeness of it all, so that it is now a part of memory exquisite and beautiful. There is an immeasurable dearness attached to the memory of the hours spent in sweet communion with those one loves, that makes all the hours richer and lovelier. It has been a week of great revealment to me, the disclosing of the hidden mysteries of the lovesource, the achievement of the real understanding of the love of man for man and of woman for man. I shall never pass through a lovelier experience than that which surrounds me now in the love of these boys for me, of my love for them, of your love for me and mine for you, and of Helen Campbell's love for us all. The mother love, father love[,] sister and brother love. The very God love that emanates from this dearest woman. The universe cannot help but dance playfully before us with such love.

Let me have a word now and then when you can. I know you are up to the ears in work and think of you continually, digging your way out. Harlan Ober and myself are guests of Miss Drew for our rooms and H.C.'s for our meals, for an indefinite time, so continue to address me here for at least a month. I shall go from here to Lewiston for a week before going to Boston to look the ground over for winter living. I think I have told you that I am about decided on Boston for the winter. Since my exhibition which was a fine success in all ways ($90-realized) many advantages have come to me. Several

people of influence and position have offered me their services
to help me get established and so all told I think Boston it will
be. Living is cheaper and the entrée into professional and social
circles is already established and this is necessary for success.
One lady friend of Helen C. offers to get me an exhibition in
Philadelphia, also a studio at Mrs. [Ole] Bull's⁸ in Cambridge
is at my disposal. These are some of the things waiting. I could
get to Maine easily for a winter sketching trip if I wished; would
have the constant association of the boys, of Bloomfield, enough
in itself[,]could run down to see Helen C., also easy to go to
N.Y. if I need to. So I shall try the winter in Boston I'm pretty
sure now, and develop my work there. I think you will heartily
approve in the face of the prospects, and one must take a
certainty in preference to an uncertainty. Mrs. Bull's circle
would be open to me of course. It is not necessary to enumerate
the other good things that promise good fortune. I shall go on
resting here after the strain of the summer. A cold after you
left has kept me under normal a little[,]not to speak of a painful
strain of the muscles of the abdomen while wheeling a barrel
of water. These two indispositions have stopped my hard work
and now I need do nothing but recuperate. My love for you
and all the love of us all is yours always. We talk of you daily.
Yesterday Helen C. said "I think Horace is snowed under with
work, that he hasn't written you of late"—In two minutes came
your last letter.

Wiksell and his wife came over one day from Hampton—the
last day of my exhibition and I was happy to have them see it
at its best.

Love.
Marsden Hartley

Green Acre
Eliot Maine

Don't forget me on the manuscript of "Do you help me to live,"
that is, if you feel like letting me have it.

Undated letter, postmarked September 11, 1907, Portsmouth, N.H.

My Dear Horace

Your letter came to me today at Green Acre. Yes I feel it is to be Boston. I do need you—more than you have idea of— but it does not appear to be New York yet. Some time it will surely be Philadelphia and then my joy will be limitless. Love to you from all of us.

M. Hartley
Portsmouth P.O.

Write me any time you can. I love your words dearly.

Undated post card, postmarked September 11 [year illegible, 1907?]

Dear Horace,

Harlan Ober, Miss Drew and myself are in Dover, N.H. for an hour. I do not like this town. It looks forlorn and desolate. Not the charm of Portsmouth by any means. Love to you my dear Horace.

[no signature]

Undated postcard, postmarked September 13, 1907, Dover, N.H.

Just a few words my dear brother out of the exquisite night. The white path across the heavens was never milkier than now and the crickets are singing the fullest out of sheer joy. I see you sitting buried up to the ears in work and wish I were there and could do things for you. Who knows, may be one of these days I will be proving of real service to you instead of posing on a pedestal, a mere ornament. I shall glory in the day and bid it hasten. Helen Campbell is so glad for your messages and is glad for your love for me and for her. We are both happy beyond words in it, and every word you send to either is shared with highest joy. I am sorry, more than you know, that the winter does not bid strong for New York—I need you now as never before. The mere thought of you is as a torch to the fire and it seems as if I must let all things go and get near to you. You are my dearest brother because you are nearest me. All are near and dear but none touch my heart closer than you do. This is why I say I need you as never before. From morning till the night is on, you traverse the earth wherever I go, and I seem to be talking to you as intimately as if you were actually in my presence. Your messages are flashlights across the deserts. Send them all as you can. Love unbounded goes to you out the heart of my heart, out of the heart of my soul. Love again. Always love.

Marsden H.

Undated letter, postmarked September 13, 1907, Eliot, Maine.

My Dear Horace,

When I get into Portsmouth I think instantly of you and all these streets are dear because we walked them together and it is a kind of commemoration to drop the cards to you as I do. I think of you constantly and all my joys include you because of your kind thoughts for me or rather just because of yourself. Don't deny me any word when you have the time. Love—love.

M. Hartley

Undated postcard, postmarked September 14 [year illegible, 1907?], Portsmouth, N.H.

My Dear Horace

I want to say to you that my dear brother Harlan Ober leaves here on Friday for a trip to Washington and intends stopping over on his way back to see you in Philadelphia. He wants to know you, wants your love because you have his and hopes he will find his place in your esteem. You will find no truer fellow walking the earth, you will find him tremendously spiritual but walking with his feet square on the ground. I am having exquisite experiences with his love for me and his shows of brotherly tenderness and affection. He stands high among men and cannot be over estimated. Helen Campbell loves him as I do, because he loves us both and we know the quality and calibre of his man stuff. You were an inspiration to him during his little experience with you and he wants a good taste of you. If you have any time to spare give it to him and he will love you for it as well as for yourself. He is an admirable lover of humanity and devotes himself to it. He is by faith a teacher of the Baha'i religion but this will have no part in the intercourse I think. I do not intend to convey the idea that I am under rating this part of the fellow. I do not. It is the beauty of him, because he is a universal soul and seeks universality. I do not know that this preliminary note is in the least necessary. It may be entirely superfluous on the face of the man's own recommendations. He is my brother and I love him deeply. Therefore I think he can be your brother and wants to be. We are having divinest of times he and I with Helen Campbell, taking our meals, and rooming at Miss Drew's house as her guest. He will return to us after the Washington trip and we shall wait with eagerness to hear of his happy time with you. Your card came today and shall expect the manuscript tomorrow. I thank you deeply from my heart. I shall hold these essences of you as my closest treasures, my dearest possessions. I love the love that gives them to me so freely. Love to you my dear Horace. Let it help to smoothe out the work tangles.

Marsden Hartley

Undated letter, postmarked September 18, 1907, Eliot, Maine.

I am supremely happy my dearest Horace to hold to me that precious manuscript "Do you help me to live." You don't know the gift you confer upon me in sending me this. It is the next thing to having you actually by my side, as when I touch it, instantly you speak, move and have splendid being with me. I think you are not enough aware how you do help the world to live. I think you may not be fully conscious of the tremendous influence emanating over the earth whenever you pass or your words pass. I count myself heaven blessed with your precious love and ask no more than to walk on throughout the exquisite days with you and to have concourse with your heart and soul daily, hourly, and in every moment waking or sleeping. It is enough that you vibrate through my being. It is enough that you call me brother, friend, lover. I am satisfied to walk with you on the one side and God all about and between us. You enrich my life with greatest beauty and the blossoms along the way and the songs out of the air are sweeter because you are in them as I look and listen. Heaven spreads itself out lavishly over men and all the earth is glad,—because you love it and because we love each other. Thanks and again thanks for your manuscript and for your love. Take the fulness of mine to your heart and let it bloom there that I may beautifully bloom there and become that which I must become through your love, through all men's love and all women's love.

Marsden Hartley
Sep 20, 1907

Portsmouth, N.H.
Tuesday

My Dearest Horace. At the usual place with my dear friend
Edith Howell, one of the dearest girls living that you must one
day know. She is at Green Acre for a week with us. She may
some time call on you in Phila. We both send our love.

Marsden Hartley

Undated postcard, postmarked October 1 [year illegible, 1907?].

My dear Horace

My love to you from Portsmouth. Have just left Edith Howell who goes on to Bangor, Pa. If she ever calls on you, it will make her happy. You will love her as all we boys do. She is strong and tender, loving and noble. My love to Helen Campbell and all the rest to you. The sun shines so deliciously on the pavement and the children's shouts ring sweet.

Marsden Hartley

Undated postcard, postmarked October 5 [year illegible, 1907?], Portsmouth, N.H.

My Dear Horace

A word to you along with those to my dearest Mother Helen. It makes me happy when I think of you together enjoying each other to the full. I am happy in her absence because you are happy in her presence and her return to me will be so sweet because you have been together. I have been peculiarly conscious this past two days of the happiness of some one most dear to me. I think it may be yours I feel in the air. I am with you and your plain song is heard and loved.

Love   Love.

Marsden Hartley

Undated postcard, postmarked October 12 [year illegible, 1907?], Portsmouth, N.H.

My Dear Horace—

Enclosed is a card from a new subscriber to The Conservator which explains itself. The dollar was collected by Miss Drew and given to Mother Helen Campbell while you were here, so if you have this name on your list you can change the address to the one given on the card.

I am still in Eliot, keeping house in Mother Helen's rooms until further developments. Miss Drew has decided not to go south and will be in Boston this winter instead, so she will be here for a little longer. Somewhere about the 7th or 10th of November I want to go to Lovell for a few days to do some sketching for winter work, as about that time the autumn color will have left and the rich sober yet powerful color will have come upon the mountains. I think nature is never quite so dramatic as when she is bared to the brow and shows her face in sturdy acceptance of the coming cold and dreariness, with the "cool unfolding" purples and the deep greens that mingle sedately with it, set off here and there with sketches of mauve white or cream gray. I do not believe there is anything more artistic in all of nature's display and I personally have a great preference for this scheme of coloring and its varying scales of harmony in tone. It is like a strong resonant octave out of Chopin, out of Grieg. One person lately told me that to her my painting is on the plane of Grieg's music which is a little complimentary, and something to live up to.

Au Revoir dear Horace. My love to Anne Montgomerie[9][,] Gertrude[10] and my Mother Helen. Unceasing love to you.

Marsden

Undated letter, postmarked October 29, 1907, Portsmouth, New Hampshire.

Phila
Oct 30 '07

Hartley old boy:

I send you my love. Helen Campbell is still with us. God knows, she has been bad sick: shaken to the roots. But the tree was not made to fall this time. I have not sent you alarming messages. She has not been laid up. But she was in danger. Her nerve saved her. Her gut. She just said "no" to death—& that's all there was about it. Death slunk away. You are always with us. We take you for granted. I am not sure Helen's close-by view of me confirms her faith. I have not posed for her. I am as I am. If you can see through my faults far enough to see any virtues, lucky me. I would give up the search myself. But I see things myself in my friends & that is all I need. I don't need to be loved. But I do need to love.—Well, old stocking[?]: I wish you were here. I would like to have you loaf about here & in Camden with me. We could get much out of life together. No matter. That will come, too—Tell me about your work. I was never harder worked myself but I make no money. I haven't made a cent since I came back from Boston. The financial luck all flies the other way. No matter again. To hell with financial luck. To heaven with love.

Horace

My Dear Horace,

Your great letter came yesterday and makes me happy. I have
thought mighty hard for my dear Mother Helen and I am glad
she is on the high road if even she cannot yet be roughing it
as she likes. I have longed to be near her in the body that I
might add my service to her needs. God wants her with us all
so much and she shall not go out of our sight for long to come.
Her real work is on the commencement and is going to get done
and royally too. God bless you all for your loving care over
her. I will write soon. Love Horace, to each and all.

Marsden

Undated postcard, postmarked November [day illegible] 1907,
Portsmouth, N.H.

My Dear Horace,

The old hat and the new love reached me and I am glad of them. Things go badly here and the N.Y. project is knocked in the head and so here I am—beached—waiting for a tide. I expect to have a sale of potboilers at the Metaphysical Club for two weeks beginning the 15th of April—I hope to pull out a few dollars from this to get me out of town and to the mountains for the spring color which I have never seen as yet. I very frequently question the painting business at these rates —but I shall go on some longer and see how it turns out—it cannot always be bad—though it certainly gripes at this stage of the game.

But never mind it's all right—if the world isn't encouraging in art it is most encouraging in love and I am mighty glad for love.

I suppose you're up to your neck in moving. It is not a joyful task but has to get done—I wish I were there to help you.

Love always to you dear Horace.

Marsden Hartley

3 Willow St. [Boston]

Undated letter, postmarked April 8, 1908.

Shout Horace Traubel—shout for Hartley's success—I'm discovered so they say and am on my way. Desmond Fitzgerald[,][11] owner of Monets, Sisleys, Boudins[,] D'Espagnats[,] etc. etc.[,] has bought my "Maine Blizzard" and wants another later—$200 is the price and it's to be in my hand today. Enneking[12] says splendid things of my work, applauds my "power, and tragic sense." Philip Hale[13] art critic passes upon them with praise offers to write me up if I give a show, and wants me to send them to the "Salon Independents"[14] early next year: Fitzgerald wants me to get away to the mountains and paint freely and have no worries over the future, sees in my work a new note in art and that I am getting at the secret of the mountains as no one else has. My "blizzard" goes into his house with the fine Monets etc. He took me down to Cape Cod yesterday to meet Dodge Macknight, that most uniquely original painter in America: D.M. was most gracious, said fine things of my work and being a man of few words— this means much. He offered his congratulations on the success in my work and calls the "blizzard" a "<u>fine</u> <u>picture</u>," and invites me to visit him at any time. I am to go to California next fall for perhaps a year to paint in that vividly glowing country and to attune my senses to livelier color. So I'm on my way Horace and I know you're glad. Your love with the rest has kept the dark days bright and will now make the bright days brighter. Love to you always.

Marsden Hartley

3 Willow St. [Boston]

I go to Maine in a week to remain until November.

Undated letter, postmarked May 8, 1908.

Carnival of Autumn, oil on canvas, 1905–09
(Courtesy Museum of Fine Arts, Boston)

Well, beloved Horace, how are you anyhow? I've thought of you much oftener than you know and have wanted the dear times over again with you and (if it were not vain) to tell you of my recent good luck. It's been quite an Arabian Night's tale all round and doesn't seem real even yet. All through the good words of Philip Hale who seemed to be a deal interested in them (my pictures) I went to see him first to ask if I might show the stuff to him and found him a most genuine sort of man and invited me cordially to take my things up to his studio, which I did in a few days. He pronounced them very distinctive and most individual and to give his own words—"a *fine insanity*" about them which pleased him—and by 'insanity' he explained himself as meaning a strong insistence upon the personal interpretation of the subjects chosen—suggested that I send them over to the Independent Salon in Paris early next year. Then I took them to the Rowlands Gallery to show them there and Enneking walked in—said good morning to me and asked Rowlands whose the pictures were and R. said this young man's—whereupon Enneking turned with great surprise and said he had no idea that I was doing such powerful work. He said there was in it the mysticism of Böcklin with the dignity of [Puvis de] Chavannes. He was most free in his praises—likewise Desmond Fitzgerald who bought my "Maine Blizzard"—a man who owns the finest collection of modern pictures in New England—with a bunch of Monets, Sisleys, Boudins and others with a stack of pictures of that brilliant and unique genius Dodge Macknight—Fitzgerald took me down to Cape Cod to spend the day at Macnight's to show my things —and MacKnight who is a most critical and conservative man said "I want to congratulate you on that fine picture, Mr. Hartley" (the blizzard) which praise I value more than all coming from an artist whose work appeals to me more than any other I know in America. Fitzgerald discovered him and set him going twenty years ago and is buying his things right along. F. encourages my going to California which I so much want to do next year. Maybe I'll get there. But I thought a lot about you all Saturday & wished I could be with you and picked a sprig of lilac blooming perennial for the thought of you all I love and if I had thought earlier would have sent you on a sprig for the dinner. Had a dear little while with Mosher[16] in Portland. He is most lovable and I am most glad for his kindnesses and shows of affection toward me for I think he really trusts me, and his trust is love I believe.

Let's have a dear old line when you can. I shall miss those heavenly whiles with you this summer. They were greater than all others and will be rightfully missed.

I throw a kiss to you across these isolated hills and with it all my love in lilac time.

Love to you always.

                                        Marsden Hartley

North Lovell
Maine

Undated letter, postmarked June 2, 1908.

Bridgton, Maine—

Walked over from N. Lovell return this afternoon—32 miles in all—going through the deep woods stripped to the waist ready for every stray breeze—jumped into a brook on the way and cooled myself up to the ears and then dressed and started on. Wish you were here to go it with me. Have been getting rations to keep camp with. Wish you could come up here but I know you love the dear crowd too well. So do I—but one can't have all things in the hills. Love always, M. Hartley

Undated postcard, postmarked [month and day illegible] 1908

My Dear Horace

I am in New York. I want so much to see you. Will you let me know when you come back this way. Got some Conservators yesterday forwarded from Lewiston and it was good to see your hand again. Love to you. Please let me know. I know some artists would like to know you—Robert Henri—John Sloan[17]—both big men.

Love, Marsden H.

N.Y. 202 W. 81st Street

Undated postcard, postmarked March 11, 1909

My Dear Horace.

I'm terribly disappointed not to see you—I rested in peace thinking you had my address as I got The Conservator day before yesterday. I wanted you to see my pictures and would have given you a special show since you won't be here until after it is over. It seems to be a curious work of fate that you have never seen my work—Once it was my fault—now it is nobody's—The artists have given me high very flattering praises and that I am to have a show in N.Y. is due wholly to the enthusiasm of these men—all expenses being paid by the Society in whose gallery I am to make my N.Y. debut tomorrow.[18] I only hope it will be so I can be here for the Whitman dinner,[19] but I cannot say. It seems to me the last Conservator is about as beautiful as you have done—at least it seems to thrill me more at this time—maybe because I have gone alone so long and suddenly find myself surrounded with love[,] I mean more love—and sympathy. I wouldn't from choice have missed you for worlds and worlds, because it would have been good for me to see you.

Love to you.
Marsden Hartley

202 West 81st St. [New York]

Undated letter [May 8, 1909].

Ticket for Whitman dinner

Montreal
July 22nd '10
(485 Elm Ave)

Say, Hartley, dear comrade, I'm here for a few weeks working on my books & trying to catch up with myself. My heart said to me this morning: send your hello to Hartley. So I obey my heart. You are always cherishable & always cherished. You give me great delight. You too have your problem & will work it out. There is a beyond. In that beyond you will figure vitally & triumphantly. I do not doubt it. I will write again for sure.

Horace

Facsimile of Marsden Hartley letter

Where are you dear Horace—out with the world crowd
somewhere—you who love it so—I hope you are—I wish I
too could be with it—It is the incongrous thing in my entire
life, this isolation—the thing I do not want for myself—
My work requires it—but I myself have no need or use for it—
Perhaps once on a time I found isolation imperative—I think
all chrysalids do—all embryos go for the under side of the
leaf in the time of body-changes—preparing for the final
reassertion—resurrection—the establishment of the entity. But
now I've come up to the outside of my casements. I'm in need
of getting & keeping close to the human body & heart and
this touching of trees & rocks—this dabbling in clouds
& moonrays leaves one cold—My heart is warm and wants
the warmth of the world heart close to it. I think once these
ecstasies may have been too much—but now that I am big
and up to size—I find they don't please me much—I can take
it all in proudly—and hold out for more—

I fancy you are hobo-ing about with Wiksell after custom
of old—I hope so—I so wish we could do the Portsmouth &
York Beach Street over again—maybe we will some of these
summers—I hope for it strongly for it is beautiful—How lucky
you must feel to get The Conservator up to date and a little
ahead even—the lagging behind is bad for any of us—we must
keep with the moment and with a little beyond it I believe[,]
anticipate the unknown and be ready for it on its arrival—It
is better to be walking about with new young stars in one's
hand than fumbling over old meteors—sodden in the earth—I
like myself to dawdle about among constellation clusters and
to rub their dust on me than to wallow in ashes. Anyhow, love
to Wiksell—I would so love to be with him. As for you I think

I would throw my arms around you & kiss you just because you are my brother whom I have not seen for long. Love to you. Write the promised line to me soon. I jumped high with joy in my soul when I found your letter here in the hills.

Marsden H.

North Lovell
Maine
Oxford Co.

Undated letter, postmarked July 23, 1910.

485 Elm Ave
Montreal
Aug 13th '10

Yes, I do think of you always dear Hartley & always with love. I do not forget the old days. How often Greenacre & Portsmouth come back into my heart with precious reminders of fraternal meetings there. I can't believe that the things we started there in you & in us—in you & in me—can ever lose their pertinence or cease to be a joy. I am here with friends. I came to loaf but have worked every day since my arrival. Mosher & Wiksell are to join us on Monday.

Horace

Dear Anne Traubel.

    I am sending you with this the extra plate out of the El Greco book which we got together. I think you will be glad to have it and I am as glad to give it to you. I have but lately arrived at the office after leaving your house—I reach here feeling so well & happy—you are health and joy to the tired body and peace to the soul—one grows and blooms in the presence of you—one feels like something big & beautiful when you are around—It is too soon to see the real meaning of this visit to Phila. but I know it is big—and I knew it would be big because I have waited so long to see you. You have been so fine a "hearsay" for so long—I have heard the others tell of you—and so these lovely whiles mean very very much to me—I shall be writing you from out the wilds of the north and it will be good to hear you speak softly and inspiringly out of Camden. God bless you. God bless Gertrude.

                                      Marsden Hartley

Undated letter [no envelope]

Dear Anne Traubel.

Your beautiful letter came last night to me here in the silences—I was happy with it and am happy with it still. It is a beautiful message for anyone to deliver, this dark man's message. I am thinking of it this morning as I sit writing you after having started a picture, done a washing which lies purifying in the sun on the grass. This hermit life which I live—curiously unlike me, does not bring me all the happiness it should[.] I am eminently social—I like the feel of others (congenial) like myself around somewhere—the trees & the birds & the running waters—the fishes lying still in the bed of the brook—I watched them as I stood rinsing my clothes in the running water[—] do not always convey their full significance to me—they do not always give me things—I lose the great purport of all silent things in the craving for the sweetest of things—companionship—I am free to confess that as yet art has never been more than love and friendship nor has it been less—some would say it has nothing to do with either of them because art is purely intellectual and has little to do with the simple emotions—However I have painted on a picture—I have attended to the needs of my body—I have washed my raiment white and purified it with the waters of the hills & skies—as the fish lay still under them in the process of spawning for procreation and these things were not enough—the heart calls for more—the heart needs that which is closer akin to it and so I am feeling the loneliness in the presence of these beautiful unhuman things—there is too much peace, there is too much indifference[,] too much of supremacy of mighty things—things that know not what it is to be human—that are conscious only of the great energy in them over which they have no direction—there is health in the presence of them but there is not peace with the lonliness among them—I do not urge them to go from me—I do not crave to go from them—I desire only a human hand to touch[,] a big broad shoulder to brush by—a wondrous deep souled eye to look into—a smile to be conscious of upon a face somewhere near—Then the ceaseless rushing of the waterfall—the casual note of a wandering bird[,] the flicker of the yellow butterfly across the young grass around me—all these would have the right meaning—and I would feel the pulse & secret of all that is. These are the emotions that fill me here as the sun is nearly noon high and the sky afloat with wandering clouds—

I've been planting my garden too this morning previous to painting—planting wax beans—having already sowed early peas—beets—lettuce, romaine, and in between them patches of zinnias—marigolds straw-flowers & poppies—also dipper gourds—which if they materialize will offer much in the way of health & pleasure—planting is later up here necessarily as the conditions are different from those of the south—your south—& harvests are likewise deferred—so that garden stuffs do not arrive until August & September—with the exception of early peas—   I like that foreword of yours for the Ingersoll book of Mosher's[20]—I shall be sending for it soon, as curious as it may seem I know almost nothing of him—I like the sound & feeling of Toward Humanity—It sounds so much more beautiful than toward heaven or toward anything else and I like anybody who makes that his keynote—Tomorrow is Whitman dinner day isn't it—I'd like in many ways to be there—not for the dinner or the speeches but for several that I know whom I would love to be with awhile and doubtless some whom I do not know and would know well—Wm. Gable[21] I should like to see—Mildred Bain[22]—I had thought to write Gable as I suppose he will be there—Horace also—much has intervened to prevent but I shall be doing so before long.

I thank you for the beautiful letter—for the message of the dark man with the white soul—& shall think of it often—It is indeed enough to be kind—without discrimination—I like the feeling of being so, myself. Do write me soon again. Love to Horace & yourself.

Marsden H.

Undated letter, postmarked May 31, 1911, North Lovell, Maine

Dear Anne Traubel.

I have good news this morning—and I think it is for you too—a letter from Alfred Bartlett in Boston who through me knows the dear sailor fellow John Wilson—writes this morning a gladdening letter stating that Wilson went home a free man this week—He had promised (dreadful thought) to return to the ship the following day & re-enlist & through a long talk with Bartlett & another dear fellow Lange he changed his resolutions[,] went back to the ship & struck himself off the list and took the next morning train for Maine. This is why I am especially jubilant this sunny morning in Baltimore—and why Pleasant Street—on which I am stopping & where I write will for always be one of the pleasantest streets I know of—I feel as if I and the world had been given some wondrous sweet gift—to be sure only a man's soul & body—but somehow it seems enough to me. It is selfish joy too for I feel directly my own gladness in this news & yet I know the world on land will not be sorry for the decisions and I shall be eternally glad. I will see that you meet him one day—It might be that he will strike Phila—this some day—Anyhow I will send you his picture that you may look at the face of one who is inwardly lovely & lovable—This it is that makes me glad & the glory of those beauteous days in Phila keeps me in the light of the sun—I shall not forget them—The green book with its nice red cover glows with memories already—which will [illegible word] & cling forever about it—Love to you & Gertrude & Horace—

I intend stopping off on the way over to N.Y. to get Horace who said that he had to go over the first of the week—so I may have joy of seeing you soon again. And I long so to be off to Maine now that I know that Wilson is safe home for we have much to say to each other—and when I am there talking to him & conversing with the immensities about us both I shall think of you & be glad.

faithfully
Marsden Hartley

Undated letter, postmarked April 21, 1911, Baltimore, Md.

Hello dear Horace—I should not be so lax I know—but I've been off seeing my sailor friend John Wilson for two weeks at Norway Maine and have been back a week now. I miss him for he is a beautiful fellow. I want you to see him some day and during next winter it may happen. I am wondering what's happening with you. When you write to Gable give him my love—I shall write him a card also—and a letter some time soon. The problems of painting and house-keeping absorb me—more than I like but I have to keep at them both to make life out—If loved ones were closer at hand work would be easy—Somehow this business of one isn't big enough—Love to you. I think over those rich days with you in Phila. often. They were blessings to me. Love, Write me soon. M. H.

Undated postcard, postmarked June 26, 1911(?), North Lovell, Maine.

Dear Anne Traubel—This merely to let you know I am not far off. Arrived in N.Y. Sunday evening—It feels so good to be close to the crowd—I shall want to get over to Phila. & Camden before a great while—but not yet. Maybe by Christmas I can get over for a few days. Write me if you can & feel like it and tell Horace if he comes over to please let me know. I have the richest memories of Phila. & Camden & want always to celebrate them. A Christmas gift to myself of that sort would satisfy completely & I want to tell you about my beautiful dog who loves me so. She is in Maine now & is coming down later on, surely by Christmas. Love to all. M.H.

When you see a beautiful face think of me—I am seeing so many now.

Undated postcard, postmarked November 23, 1911, New York, N.Y.

Dear Horace.

How are you? I am not sure you have my new address—I have a nice studio now—for the first time in my life—I hope you'll find time to come and see me when you are over in New York. I have hoped to get to Phila. for a few days but I see no way clear now. I am to have an exhibition in February23— perhaps you will be over early in Feb. & would be interested in taking a look at it. I don't know that you would like it. Give my love to Anne & Gertrude & the same for yourself.

As always.
Marsden Hartley

244 West 14th St.

Undated postcard, postmarked January 16, 1912.

My dear Horace.

    I have thought of you much & loved you in my same old way. I have been here now one week from the other side—as soon as I can I will get over or wait till you come. This is at Boni's[24]—Gertrude was just in. She looks so jolly. Love to Anne & you & all others everywhere—

Marsden Hartley

351 West 15th St., N.Y.

Undated postcard, postmarked December 31, 1915.

A SONG.

First published in 1860. See note.

1

COME,[1] I will make the continent indissoluble ;
I will make the most splendid race the sun ever yet shone upon ;
I will make divine magnetic lands,
      [2]With the love of comrades,
         With the life-long love of comrades.

2

I will plant companionship thick as trees along all the rivers of
      America, and along the shores of the great lakes, and all
      over the prairies ;
I will make inseparable cities, with their arms about each other's
      necks ;
         By the love of comrades,
            By the manly love of comrades.

3

For you these, from me, O Democracy, to serve you, ma
      femme !   10
For you ! for you, I am trilling these songs,
      In the love of comrades,
         In the high-towering love of comrades.

NOT HEAVING FROM MY RIBB'D BREAST ONLY.

First published in 1860.

NOT heaving from my ribb'd breast only ;
Not in sighs at night, in rage, dissatisfied with myself ;
Not in those long-drawn, ill-supprest sighs ;
Not in many an oath and promise broken ;
Not in my wilful and savage soul's volition ;
Not in the subtle nourishment of the air ;

[1] "Come" added in 1867.
[2] Lines 4, 5, 8, 9, 12, 13, added in 1867. With these exceptions this poem
is composed of verses 13, 14 and 15 of the 5th poem in "Calamus" Edition
of 1860, beginning
"States !
Were you looking to be held together by lawyers?" See page 469.

Page from Marsden Hartley's copy of Leaves of Grass

NOTES

1.   Dr. Percival Wiksell, of Boston, was a dentist, friend of Traubel and Thomas Bird Mosher (see note 16) and shared with them great enthusiasm for the writings of Walt Whitman. Traubel often visited Wiksell in Boston, and on these occasions Mosher would often come down from his home in Portland, Maine, to join them. Hartley was included in these meetings when he was living in Boston during the winter of 1908.

2.   *The Conservator* was the monthly journal devoted to progressive literary and social ideas that Traubel started in 1890 and edited more-or-less singlehandedly until his death in 1919. The periodical did not continue beyond that year. Although Traubel founded it as an organ of the Ethical Culture movement, his gradually broadening concerns, particularly in Whitman, gave *The Conservator* great appeal among intellectuals.

3.   Traubel used the ecclesiastical term "Collects" for some of the short, pointed essays that he wrote for *The Conservator*. From time to time he would issue these as pamphlets under the *Conservator* imprint.

4.   The poem by Hartley to which Traubel refers was not found among the letters, nor has it been identified. However, Hartley seems to have been almost as serious about writing poetry as he was about painting.

5.   Helen Stuart Campbell (1839–1918), of Boston, was a friend of Traubel and author of children's books and works on the subject of women and social reform. Her works include *Prisoners of Poverty* (1888), *Women Wage Earners* (1893), and *Household Economics* (1896).

6.   Charlotte Perkins (Stetson) Gilman (1860–1935), a writer and lecturer, was deeply concerned with social justice and women's suffrage. Author of such books as *Concerning Children* (1900) and *Human Work* (1904), she also edited a women's rights periodical, *The Forerunner*, and wrote what Hartley

called "poetry of the dry kind." He remembered her as
"tall [and] angular physically[,] hard looking and very vital
mentally." (Peter Doyle and the Whitman Group," unpub-
lished manuscript. Yale Collection of American Literature,
Beinecke Rare Book and Manuscript Library, Yale University.)

7.   Green Acre, located on the edge of the Piscataqua River
at Eliot, Maine, was a retreat where figures interested in
transcendental ideas, socialism, suffragist causes, and mystical
religion came together for mutual interchange in a rural setting.
Through Mosher, Hartley got a job there erecting tents in
exchange for room and board during the summer of 1907.

8.   Wife of an opthamologist, Mrs. Ole Bull (1850–1911) was
an author and translator. A resident of Cambridge,
Massachusetts, she also had a summer home near Green Acre.
The exhibition which netted Hartley $90 was held there in
1907. Hartley recalled that Mrs. Bull "maintained a summer
residence just off the side of Greenacre itself beyond the hotel,
where she housed several swamis such as Vivikenanda,
Abedmanda, and Sister Nivedita. She was swamped in their
beliefs, and was yogi-ed out of her will. . . . " ("Peter Doyle and
the Whitman Group.")

9.   Anne Montgomerie Traubel was Horace's wife, and like
him she was keenly interested in Whitman. She served as an
agent for the Mosher Books.

10.   Gertrude Traubel (1897–   ), daughter of Anne and Horace
Traubel, was trained as a singer and taught and performed in
Philadelphia and its environs. Through her interest in
Whitman, she transcribed and edited some of her father's later
records of the poet's utterances and was instrumental in
having a reprint made of *The Artsman,* a periodical Traubel
helped to edit.

11.   Desmond Fitzgerald (1846–1926), a civil engineer, was also
a critic, collector, and writer on art. A resident of Brookline,
a suburb of Boston, his books include a biography of Dodge
Macknight (1916).

12. John Joseph Enneking (1841–1916), a painter, studied in Munich and Paris, then returned to New England, settling in Hyde Park, Massachusetts. His style ranged variously from Luminism to Impressionism.

13. Philip Hale (1865–1931) was an artist, art critic, and historian of art; he was the author of, among other books, *The Madonna* (1908), *Great Portraits* (1909), and *Jan Vermeer* (1913).

14. This was undoubtedly a reference to the Salon des Indépendants, Paris, an annual unjuried exhibition popular with more advanced artists.

15. Dodge Macknight (1860–1950), a watercolorist active in New England, was one of the first Americans to adopt a highly colored Impressionist palette. He had spent fourteen of his earlier years abroad where he became acquainted with Impressionism and the more vibrant style of Van Gogh. In later life, when his style seemed less controversial, he became popular in the Boston art world.

16. Thomas Bird Mosher (1852–1953) was, like Traubel and Wiksell, a dedicated Whitmanite. He was a publisher, by profession, issuing fine limited editions of literary works, both American and English, often designed in the tradition of William Morris. Based in Portland, Maine, he met Hartley when the two were together on a boat sailing for that city.

17. Hartley had come into contact with Henri, Sloan, and other members of "The Eight" in 1909, apparently through Maurice Prendergast. That group did not respond very favorably to Hartley's work, but he continued to profess admiration for Henri. Both Henri and Sloan became friendly with Traubel in due course, being drawn together by a common interest in Whitman and progressive social ideas.

18. This is a reference to the one-man show Alfred Stieglitz offered Hartley at the Little Galleries of the Photo-Secession ("291") May 8–18, 1909.

19.   Undoubtedly, this is a reference to one of the annual dinners sponsored by the Walt Whitman Fellowship.

20.   Hartley is referring to Robert G. Ingersoll's book, *Toward Humanity*, which Mosher published in 1908. Anne Montgomerie Traubel selected the passages for publication and wrote a brief foreword.

21.   A resident of Altoona, Pennsylvania, William F. Gable (1856–1921) was the proprietor of the leading department store in that city and a great friend of Traubel. He was a noted collector of coins, prints, books, manuscripts, and autographs.

22.   Mildred Bain was, like her husband Frank, a close friend and admirer of Traubel. She wrote the first biography of Traubel, published in New York in 1913.

23.   Undoubtedly a reference to Hartley's second one-man show at "291," February 7–26, 1912.

24.   This is probably a reference to the Washington Square Bookshop, New York, operated by Albert and Charles Boni. They were friends of Traubel and published Mildred Bain's *Horace Traubel* (1913) and the second American printing of Traubel's book, *Chants Communal*, in 1914.